First published in 2013 by
Liberties Press
140 Terenure Road North | Terenure | Dublin 6W
Tel: +353 (1) 405 5703
www.libertiespress.com | info@libertiespress.com

Trade enquiries to Gill & Macmillan Distribution
Hume Avenue | Park West | Dublin 12
T: +353 (1) 500 9534 | F: +353 (1) 500 9595 | E: sales@gillmacmillan.ie

Distributed in the United States by
Dufour Editions | PO Box 7 | Chester Springs | Pennsylvania | 19425

Distributed in the UK by
Turnaround Publisher Services
Unit 3 | Olympia Trading Estate | Coburg Road | London N22 6TZ
T: +44 (0) 20 8829 3000 | E: orders@turnaround-uk.com

ISBN: 978-1-907593-23-9
2 4 6 8 10 9 7 5 3 1
A CIP record for this title is available from the British Library.

Cover design by Ros Murphy
Internal design by Liberties Press
Printed by Bell & Bain Ltd

The publishers gratefully acknowledge
financial assistance from the Arts Council.

Praise for Gabriel Fitzmaurice

'Fitzmaurice stoutly ───── ites the characters, situations and lively peculiarities of Moyvane, County Kerry, especially resplendently in [his] sonnets.'

Ray Olson, *Booklist* (US)

'Fitzmaurice is an engaging writer with a sound grip of form and a traditional base. He favours the sonnet and is able to manipulate this challenging form very effectively.'

Angela Topping, *Orbis* (UK)

'Like Kavanagh, [Fitzmaurice] makes his own importance from the habitual. There's a cycle of sonnets that lights up love and memory and the daily miracle of Moyvane in Kerry . . . . This poised, rhythmic performance is pub-full of lore and passion.'

Mary Shine Thompson, *Sunday Independent*

'Gabriel Fitzmaurice's new book offers sonnets through which run the classic tension between pleasure and instruction.'

James J. McAuley, *Irish Times*

'[Fitzmaurice] is a master of the sonnet form.'

Eugene O'Connell, *Southword*

A Middle-aged Orpheus

LOOKS BACK
AT HIS LIFE

New and Selected Sonnets
Gabriel Fitzmaurice

For Fintan O'Toole and Clare Connell
le grá

Contents

Acknowledgements   11

Introduction by Fintan O'Toole   13

Moyvane   21

The Playman   22

Gaeltacht   23

May Dalton   24

Alzheimer's Disease   25

Lassie   26

Scorn Not the Ballad   27

To Martin Hayes, Fiddler   28

To a Guitar   29

The Fiddle Master   30

A Middle-aged Orpheus Looks Back at his Life   31

A Wrenboy's Farewell   32

To Pádraig Pearse   33

Dan Breen   34

A Windfall   35

Munster Football Final 1924   36

An Irishman Salutes the Queen*   37

Mam   38

Granada   39

On First Meeting the Marquess of Lansdowne   40

Home   41

The Fitzs Come to Town   42

My Father Hired with Farmers at Fourteen   43

Dad   44

True Love   45

A Widower   46

In Memory of My Father   47

God Bless the Child   48

A Bedtime Story   49

Poem for John   50

Listening to *Desperados Waiting for a Train*   51

Sick Child   52

Table Quiz   53

To My Son as He Leaves Home   54

To My Daughter, Pregnant   55

On Becoming a Grandfather*   56

My Girlfriends Now Are Other Children's Mamas*   57

Sonnet to Brenda   58

Just To Be Beside You*   59

A Valentine in Recessionary Times*   60

The Teacher   61

On Being Appointed Principal Teacher of Moyvane
National School   62

Before the Word 'Fuck' Came to Common Use   63

Would You Believe   64

A Catholic Speaks Out*   65

In Extremis   66

Knockanure Church   67

On Hearing Johnny Cash's *American Recordings*   68
Homage to Thomas MacGreevy   69

Books by Gabriel Fitzmaurice   71
Biographical Note   75

* denotes new sonnets

Acknowledgements

Acknowledgement is due to the publishers below where these sonnets were first published in the following books:

The Village Sings (Story Line Press, Oregon, Peterloo Poets, Cornwall, and Cló Iar-Chonnachta, Conamara, 1996).

A Wrenboy's Carnival: Poems 1980-2000 (Wolfhound Press, Dublin, Peterloo Poets, Cornwall, 2000).

I and the Village (Marino Books, Dublin, 2002).

The Boghole Boys (Marino Books, Cork, 2005).

Twenty-one Sonnets (Salmon Poetry, Cliffs of Moher, 2007).

Poems of Faith and Doubt (Salmon Poetry, Cliffs of Moher, 2011).

The new sonnets have been published in *Poetry Ireland News*, *Quadrant* (Australia) and *The Clifden Anthology* and have been broadcast on *Sunday Miscellany* (RTÉ Radio 1), *Playback* (RTÉ Radio 1) and *In Conversation With Weeshie Fogarty* (Radio Kerry).

Deep and Narrow, High and Hard

Poems are like rivers. If the banks are soft and low, the water will spread wide and shallow. But if the banks are hard and high, the water has to go deep and narrow. Thus it is with poetic form. It can be soft and loose, allowing words and thoughts to cover a lot of ground. Or it can be hard and tough, forcing the stream through a well-defined strait but also allowing that force to carve out hidden depths.

Gabriel Fitzmaurice has always been a poet of the deep and narrow. Because he is accessible and unpretentious, it is easy to overlook the truth that he is also a severe formalist. Perhaps he always sensed that the warmth and affection of his relationship with his native village, Moyvane in North Kerry, his declaration that 'rooted in this place where I belong,/ I turn our common history into song', could lend themselves to easy sentiment if they are not put through the aesthetic obstacle course of tight formality. Certainly, his instinct has always been that the only really memorable way to celebrate the ordinary is to make it extraordinary by giving it a sharply defined shape. It is form that rescues the everyday from banality, that separates the beautifully quotidian from the merely mundane. It is form that turns the family photo album of the poet's memories of his parents and his children into universal pictures. It is form that, in the words of a key Fitzmaurice sonnet, 'Homage to Thomas MacGreevey', takes the 'squalid commonplace' and 'redeems its ugly hue', that raises 'living into grace'.

In that poem, Fitzmaurice presents himself as 'a poet and a Catholic' and that religious impulse – battered, angry, betrayed, beset by doubt, but still the beating heart of his imagination – is another aspect of his attraction to traditional forms. In religion, the raw intensity of feelings – the joy of birth, the grief of loss, the despair of death – is transmuted into ritual. Even as he leaves it in anger and disillusion, Fitzmaurice is shaped by that legacy: 'the ritual and all it means to me' are in his blood. Like the kids in the bleakly powerful 'In Extremis', it's all he's got. The sacraments have the rhythms and repetitions, forms and familiarities, that make grief and joy bearable. Those emotions are not banished, but they are prevented from being overwhelming: the moving sequence on his father here concludes, aptly with a direct evocation of Christ's death and resurrection: 'Who share in this last supper, wine and bread,/ Who resurrect the memory of the dead.' Fitzmaurice's muse is deeply schooled in this sacramental impulse. The sonnet is his Mass, his confessional, his baptism and his funeral.

This makes him sound rather pious, though, and nothing could be further from the feel of these poems. A good poem, like a good short story, is made from the reconciling of contradictory impulses. (Fitzmaurice's fellow North Kerryman Bryan MacMahon described the genesis of a short story as the mating of a male idea and a female idea

– the intercourse of opposites.) What makes these sonnets crackle with energy is that their orderly, ritualistic forms are assailed and sometimes subverted by two different anarchic forces.

One of these is the attraction of starkness. The sonnet, with its roots in love poetry, has a natural affinity with the ornate, the showy, the clever twist of rhyme or wit. (Fitzmaurice plays delightfully and delightedly with this tradition in 'Sonnet to Brenda'.) Here, that impulse is held in check by the poet's attraction to bareness and exposure. Perhaps his most powerful individual poem is 'Knockanure Church'. Typically, it is rooted in the real and the local – the modernist church is very close to Moyvane. And it really is, as the poem says, a shrine to austerity before that term became a weasel word: 'Bare brick, flat roof, no steeple, here I pray.' It is this severity in which Fitzmaurice feels spiritually most at home:

My God's a God who strips me in this place –
No cover here, the lines are stark and spare;
Through the years I've grown into this space
Where work of human hands raised art to prayer

This is a religious credo but also, of course, an artistic one. The lines that are stark and spare are those of the church, but also those of the poem itself – the sonnet enacts in its form the idea that it explores. And yet, even here, there is also a lovely playfulness in the poem's final rhyme of 'Chartres' and 'heart', a witty yoking together of opposites – stone and living flesh, towering public building and private seat of emotion. Within the strict form, Fitzmaurice allows himself a delightful, subtle 'ah but' – declaring a love of starkness but sounding a quiet grace note of adornment, after all. (Interestingly, he does the opposite in 'My Father Hired With Farmers at Fourteen', breaking both the sombre tone of the poem and the frame of the sonnet with the simple – but in this context daring – pendant, 'Thanks Dad.')

The other contrary impulse is considerably less refined. Fitzmaurice is a fine musician and singer, and 'Scorn Not the Ballad' is as much a part of his credo as the severity of 'Knockanure Church'. He makes the reflexive joke: 'sober as a sonnet', and indeed the poem is another lovely contradiction – a containment within the sobriety of the sonnet of the wildness and demotic energy of the ballad. He celebrates its 'rhythm, rough and rude' in lines that are themselves roughly rhythmic. But those rhythms beat against the more stately ones of the sonnet form. It is the nicely balanced tension between the two that characterises the poet.

For the paradox of tradition is that it lives only by being transformed. The great Seán Ó Riada pointed out that, in the hands of a good musician, a traditional tune is a kind of drama. The tune itself is the past, the communal, the given note. The ornamentation is the present, the individual, the imaginative impulse to find something new within the old. This is the sense in which Fitzmaurice is a traditionalist. In terms of form, he is not merely replaying and revisiting the heritage of the sonnet's "lines that rhyme and scan". He is using it, as a great singer uses an old ballad, to train and direct his own unique voice.

What is true of form, though, is equally true of content. The mark of a mature poet, of a voice achieved through a lifetime's labour, is precisely this: that the *what* is fused with the *how*, the medium is indistinguishable from the message. Thus, in these sonnets, there is no real difference between the way they work and the stories they contain. They function by taking what is already there and lifting it lightly into another realm. And this quiet transformation of the given is also their great theme.

The loveliest images here are all about the transfiguration of the ordinary, often through art: the three Nunan sisters becoming something else on the stage ('The Playman'); a dying woman distilling herself into the essence of a single word, honour ('May Dalton'); the child translated by reading into a parallel universe in which his bike is a cowboy horse ('Mam'). The miracle of life is that simple, ordinary, banal things – the given stuff of unglamorous existence – do sometimes turn into something else, something that has a kind of radiance. In his lovely poem in praise of the great Martin Hayes, Fitzmaurice nails his own thesis to the door of the church of art: 'All that we are given, we can use'. The fiddler has no choice but to take what he has inherited, what he sees, what he lives. But he has the choice to lift it, by the care he brings to it, into a new light. He can turn necessity into freedom: 'The tune's predestined, not the way he plays.' The same, as these poems so amply testify, is true of the poet.

Sonnets

Moyvane

Am I reading you, my native place, all wrong?
In reading you, is it myself I read?
Is the village I have turned into song
Real only as a figment of my need?
The characters I see, to other eyes
Are bogmen at home only in a drain
(What do critics do but criticise?);
They survive their critics just the same.

Which is real? I ask myself again;
Is insight a reflection of oneself?
What I make eventually of Moyvane
Is what I make eventually of myself.
What I am depends on what I see
As vision proves itself in poetry.

The Playman

for Fr. Tom Hickey

You took Moyvane, a poor, passed-over place
And showed the world a village in its grace;
You took Dev's comely lasses, sturdy lads
And walked us through the crossroads. I'm glad
I was alive in your time, growing up
In a village that played Beckett, where every pup
That hung about the Corner House had seen
The Nunans – Collette, Dympna, Gerardine –
Transform themselves, and us, upon a stage.
You rehearsed us in the spirit of the age.
Thanks to you, good Father, we learned to play
Our part in the drama of the day.
You understood your village and released
The poetry within us, playman, priest.

Gaeltacht

Here, for once, I didn't pine for home:
This was a world where language altered all;
Here Irish fitted like a poem –
In school, 'twas just a subject; here you'd fall
In love with being Irish: you were free
To learn the words of love not taught in school;
Oh! Irish was that girl at the *Céilí* –
If you could only ask her out, not make a fool
Of yourself, and dance with her all night,
You'd learn the moods of Irish on her tongue;
She smiled at you, and oh! your head was light,
You danced with her and wheeled and waltzed and swung.
We danced all night, we didn't even kiss,
But this was love, was Irish, and was bliss.

May Dalton

The last word that was left to her was 'honour',
The stroke had taken all the rest away,
The one thing the void could not take from her
Was herself, and so she used to say
'Honour! Honour! Honour!' when you addressed her,
'Honour! Honour! Honour!' while her hand
Clutched her agitation. What depressed her
Was how those closest failed to understand
'Honour! Honour! Honour!', how our beaming
Was the beaming of an adult at a child:
'Honour! Honour! Honour!' had no meaning
For any but May Dalton. So we smiled.
A single word held all she had to say;
Enclosed within this word, she passed away.

Alzheimer's Disease

'They're hanging me this evening,' Mary says,
Or else it's a transplant she must have,
But her concern's observing the Fast Days
(The cares of childhood follow to the grave);
'Am I going to Mass on Sundays?' she repeats
(How the good are frightened of their Church);
All we can do is comfort with deceit;
She's satisfied, and then begins to search
For biscuits, the indulgence of her life –
She'd eat them by the packet were she let,
A humble and obedient country wife;
Everything we tell her she'll forget,
But not the past – the past is as today
Where she was damned unless she would obey.

Lassie

At ninety years he fell into a drain –
That's what John Bradley tells me from his bed
(Hospital plays tricks on old men's brains);
But for his dog, he tells me, he'd be dead.
How fact and fiction make us what we are –
He fell at home at bedtime in the dark
(The drain was years ago outside a bar);
His faithful dog had more sense than to bark –
She lay down on her master all night long,
Licked his face and wrapped him from the cold,
And when the ambulance came to take out John,
Lassie stayed and couldn't be consoled.
She guards his house and lets no stranger through –
When there's nothing left, love finds such things to do.

Scorn Not the Ballad

Scorn not the ballad: it's the tale
Of lives like ours (and told without a fuss).
Sing it with a glass of flowing ale!
What's ours belongs to none, and all, of us.
No other verse can sing us like it does,
No other verse can wring out of the past
The strange, familiar melody that flows
Like truth from all who raise the singing glass.
Scorn not the ballad! Sing it out
In every public house, in every street;
It wasn't made for parlours – hear it shout!
Though sober as a sonnet, hear it beat.
You can't escape its rhythm, rough and rude;
You hum along not caring if you should.

To Martin Hayes, Fiddler

All that we are given, we can use;
All the notes are there for us to praise –
The tune's set out before us, yet *we* choose:
The tune evolves in playing. Martin Hayes
Susses out each note before he cues
It. Taking thought, he chooses what it says,
Weaves into the fabric his own news:
The tune's predestined, not the way he plays.

The music *is*, the fiddler's taken thought –
All our moments lead to this last *doh*,
All the options, everything that's sought:
What we hear that's played is what we know.
Holy! Holy! Holy! what is wrought!
He raises up, rubs rosin to the bow.

To a Guitar

Frowned upon by purists: rightly so –
So many have done violence to the tune;
Playing you, I've learned all I know
Of music – how it can raise or ruin.
I've seen men take up the fiddle and destroy
Everything they have in music's thrall
For music's not a thing that we enjoy –
It's a gift that, once it's granted, takes all.
In giving all, we risk all that we are,
There's no hiding when you play a jig or reel
(Even if you're strumming a guitar) –
You're nothing there but what you think and feel.
And it's worth it to make music, take that chance.
You're, either way, a partner in the dance.

The Fiddle Master: Homage to Pádraig O'Keeffe

for Eugene O'Connell

School's no place for artists who can't take
The ravages of teaching: it destroys
The soul, one full of singing, that must break
As the vision that sustained it shatters, dies.
Not so O'Keeffe, the fiddler: to survive,
He packed the whole thing in one fateful day,
The inspectors on his case, he couldn't thrive
In the classroom. So he left. O'Keeffe would play.
He played throughout Sliabh Luachra, where he taught
Music to his people, who revere
A musician and a teacher who only sought,
In return for his fiddling, his fill of beer.
It killed him in the end, this way of life,
The man who took a fiddle for his wife.

A Middle-aged Orpheus Looks Back at His Life

for Kris & Lisa Kristofferson

I took my voice to places where no man
Should take his voice and hope that it would sing.
All I wanted when I began
Was to strike up my guitar and do my thing.
Haunted from home, I sang my song
While all around forgot their words and fell;
In the underworld I blundered on
In regions where not it, but I, was hell.

I took my voice to places where no man
Should take his voice and hope that it would sing;
I paid the price in lines that rhyme and scan,
The last illusion to which singers cling
Before they yield their song up to the truth
They thought they could outsing in foolish youth.

A Wrenboy's Farewell

for Maurice Heffernan & the Moyvane Wrenboys

Farewell to winter madness, summer larks,
The show is over, we're back on firm land;
No more our torches will light up the dark,
The time has come and now we must disband.
Farewell to music, singing, dancing, rhymes,
The public show of all we are about,
This pageant that we dreamed in other times –
The show is over. Put the torches out.
The old are weary, wise in their defeat,
The young protest and wonder if they can
Revive the glory, again march down the street
Under the proud banner of Moyvane.
Go home. The show is over. The banner's furled.
We walk back up the street into the world.

To Pádraig Pearse

for Declan Kiberd

I see you, Pearse, in Dublin with your sword –
Cuchulainn (hardly!), a poser with a dream.
In the new State, our teachers often bored
Us pink with *'Ireland – How She'd Seem*
To Pádraig Pearse'. I didn't give a damn –
Those essays were for old men to offload
Their hangups at new freedom. Pearse the man
Was never taught us – teachers toed
The party line in everything they taught;
A poet like Pearse was dangerous, and so
They cast him as our conscience, and some bought
It. I didn't want to know.
They forged you in their image, and I sought
A way to write those essays and to grow.

Dan Breen

for Fintan O'Toole

'there's a great gap between a gallous story
and a dirty deed'
The Playboy of the Western World

My Fight for Irish Freedom by Dan Breen –
I read it like a Western; I'd pretend
To be a freedom fighter at thirteen –
It made a change from 'Cowboys'; I'd spend
My spare time freeing Ireland in my head,
Reliving his adventures one by one –
The policemen that he shot at Solohead,
Romance about the days spent on the run.

A nation born of romance and of blood,
Once ruled by men who killed for their beliefs,
Now a nation grown to adulthood
Losing faith in heroes, tribal chiefs.
Dan Breen is laid with the giants who held sway;
The gallous reads of dirty deeds today.

gallous: a composite word incorporating *gallant*, *callous* and *gallows*

A Windfall

for Desmond and Olda Fitzgerald

The castle – Anglo-Irish – where the knights
Held out despite the English through the years;
They fought and, when it made no sense to fight,
Turned Protestant, like many of their peers.
The Civil War. In 'twenty-two, the knight's
An enemy of the people (so they say).
Some hotheads want to burn him out; one night
He's raided by the local IRA.
The old knight in his wheelchair holds his ground
If they burn the castle, they must burn him too;
They won't kill him; they put their petrol down
And head back to the local to review
The situation. They don't return. (They're jarred).
The knight retains their petrol for his yard.

Munster Football Final 1924

Nothing polarises like a war,
And, of all wars, a civil war is worst;
It takes a century to heal the scars,
And even then some names remain accursed.
The tragedies of Kerry, open wounds –
John Joe Sheehy on the run in 'twenty four,
The Munster Final in the Gaelic Grounds:
There's something more important here than war.
John Joe Sheehy, centre forward, Republican,
Con Brosnan, Free State captain, centre field;
For what they love, they both put down the gun –
On Con's safe conduct, Sheehy takes the field.
In an hour the Kerry team will win.
Sheehy will vanish, on Brosnan's bond, again.

An Irishman Salutes the Queen

You came, you saw, you conquered, English rose,
No Caesar come to keep our people down,
You bowed to the memory of those
Who rose against your country and your crown;
The past at last forgiven, now it's time
To face the future confident that we
Can rise from hurt as, friends, in hope we climb
To live as equals, from ancient hatreds free.
For no more can hate or ignorance divide
(Oh! the bigotry in which we once were drilled),
I remember all the Irish who have died,
I bow before the English we have killed.
You came to us, a monarch dressed in green,
You understand your symbols. Welcome, Queen!

Mam

My mother wrote the meanings of hard words
In the margins of the books she'd recommend;
I coasted through those stories, and was stirred
By fantasy and romance: I'd pretend
To be what I was reading, made my bike
A cowboy horse, a hurley for a gun,
Picked a branch of hazel for a Viking
Spear; I'm sure she wondered at her son
Living out a fiction she'd prepared;
Her intention was to educate –
To spare me from a shop where if you dared
To speak your mind, customers might 'migrate'.
A grocer's wife, wary of romance,
She bought those books, and I should take my chance.

Granada

My mother should have been here, but ill health
Confined her to her bed much of her life –
That, and her lack of worldly wealth,
Her meagre store, a village grocer's wife.
She'd read about it when she'd sight to read,
Heard it sung (in English) on LP;
Confined to bed, her mind was all she'd need –
To see it in the flesh, she left to me.
Enough for her that she had heard its song;
Enough for her that, though she'd never see
Granada and all for which she longed,
Enough it was to know their poetry.
Through narrow streets, among the souvenirs,
I think of her through mingled sweat and tears.

On First Meeting the Marquess of Lansdowne

Listowel Castle, 21 April 2005

The Marquess of Lansdowne is the direct descendant of Patrick Fitzmaurice, son of Thomas Fitzmaurice, 18th Lord Kerry. Patrick was five years old when Listowel Castle, the last Fitzmaurice castle to hold out against Queen Elizabeth I, was besieged by Sir Charles Wilmot in November and December 1600. He was smuggled out of the castle upon its surrender. Patrick, 19th Lord Kerry, was subsequently captured, educated in England and raised in the Protestant faith.

'Which line do you belong to?' I don't know.
Too poor to trace, there's no record of my line.
Somewhere, somehow, long ago,
Someone, a Fitzmaurice, one of mine,
Left it all behind him and now I
Can't trace my line to castles. All I know
Is we left all that behind us, I don't know why
But know myself a poet, proudly low.
A rich man with a title finds his place
In history. It was ever so.
The rest of us are hard pressed to trace
Our great-grandparents. It's enough to know
That, rooted in this place where I belong,
I turn our common history to song.

Home

My family are dying one by one,
My uncles and my aunts – just Peg now left:
The ones who, returning to Moyvane,
Brought England with them in the way they dressed.
They'd travel home from Shannon on the bus
(We'd no cars back then to make the trip),
Though a lifetime 'over', they spoke the same as us,
Still the same old Kerry accent rough and rich.
They never lost their Kerry: they'd no need
To lose themselves in England, or to pine
For Ireland lost as they passed on their seed;
My cousins are English, and our line
Still comes home to visit: they belong,
A people and a place that still are one.

The Fitzs Come to Town

Those sultry summer nights in Dinny Mack's,
The Fitzs home from England; the whole clan
Singing, dancing, drinking for the crack.
Those nights were the talk of half Moyvane.
Musicians came and played till closing time,
The Fitzs danced their old-time sets again,
Drink flowed like talk that's loosed by beer and wine
And teens accepted shandies from the men.
Those sultry summer nights in Dinny Mack's
All were welcome among the Fitzs, who
Brought the summer with them and relaxed
Who never shirked when there was work to do.
And Dinny Mack would stand us the odd round
Saying "Tis better than the Carnival when the Fitzs
come to town".

The crack: often mistakenly Gaelicised as *'the craic'*, it means revelry, fun, high spirits

My Father Hired with Farmers at Fourteen

My father hired with farmers at fourteen –
No time for school, there were siblings to be fed;
He worked, a servant boy who farmers deemed
Barely worth their shillings and a bed.
My father hired with farmers at fourteen;
He took the boat for England when he could,
A servant boy no more, he'd not be seen
The victim of some farmer's whims and moods.
My father hired with farmers at fourteen
While I, precocious, a selfish little brat
Strutted out book learning. I was mean:
I'd never know the places Dad was at.
My father hired with farmers at fourteen;
He made damn sure his son was free to dream.
Thanks Dad.

Dad

A man before his time, he cooked and sewed,
Took care of me – and Mammy in her bed,
Stayed in by night and never hit the road.
I remember well the morning she was dead
(I'd been living up in Arklow – my first job,
I hit the road in patches coming home),
He came down from her room, began to sob
'Oh Gabriel, Gabriel, Gabriel, Mam is gone.'
He held me and I told him not to cry
(I loved her too, but thought this not the place –
I went up to her room, cried softly 'Why?'
Then touched her head quite stiffly, no embrace).
Now when the New Man poses with his kid,
I think of all the things my father did.

True Love

They didn't sleep together in the end:
'True love', Mam called it from their double bed;
Her illness made her husband her best friend.
He took no other mate when she was dead.
They didn't sleep together in the end:
From midlife on, my father slept alone;
I wonder how he felt being her best friend
But he didn't complain and stayed with her at home.
They didn't sleep together in the end:
There's more to love than self – they both knew this;
They loved enough to call each other 'friend' –
That's what it meant each night when they would kiss
Before Dad left their room to sleep alone.
True love it was. That's what kept them going.

A Widower

They thought to make you marry when she died;
Accounts of matches came from women who
Would share your life should you take one as bride,
But, constant as your love for her was true,
You lived alone for nearly thirty years
In the home you made with Mam, an invalid.
I remember once you told me over beers
The reason why you did the things you did.
You said you'd bring no other to your life
Fearing I, your only child, would be upset.
Not so, Dad: caring for your wife
You knew the love that lovers don't forget.
The others who would wed you came too late.
A love like yours would take no other mate.

In Memory of My Father

Since my father died, I've changed. It seems
That I become my father more and more;
I carry him around, awake, in dreams
Who followed me alive. Now his door
Is locked. House closed, I have my father's key;
I open the familiar, room by room –
Not just a house, it's more a memory.
The house itself must not become a tomb
So I open up the windows, light the fire,
Decide which clothes I'll give to charity
(The rest I'll burn later in a pyre),
Host a farewell for the family
Who share in this last supper, wine and bread,
Who resurrect the memory of the dead.

God Bless the Child

God bless the child that never grew to life,
Our dead embryo – not even a stillbirth –
Detached inside its mother's womb. My wife
And I can't even give it to the earth
From which life comes, returning it to dust.
I'll light a candle for it; on second thought,
I won't. I can't – to do so would be just
A sentimental gesture, a bouquet bought
At Reception on visiting my wife,
A silent touch perhaps to bring relief;
No candles then, I seek the words of life
That one, perhaps, might fertilise our grief.
Now every word upon my lips is prayer,
Pregnant with the life that we must bear.

A Bedtime Story

I want to give my children what I got –
A sign of middle age and childhood past:
'A story about Daddy – tell us what
You did when you were little – just like us.'
What survives our childhood we don't choose –
We must forgive our childhood if we can:
We cannot cite our childhood as excuse –
Hurt is not a licence to do wrong.
And so I bring my children to my past,
A past that was unhappy as 'twas good –
A story now, and so my kids have guessed
The happy ending, as indeed they should.
I tuck them in as sleep tugs at their lids.
I hope they'll wish their childhood on their kids.

Poem for John

A bucket on his head, a pretend soldier
Wearing Mammy's boots that reached above his knee. . .
He remembers this quite clearly now he's older –
The magic world he lived in, turning three.
He'd go to bed sitting on my shoulder,
His *Daddy Doodle*, oh so proud of me!
It's not that what's between us has grown colder –
To grow apart is part of being free.

I love you, son, as on the day you came
Into my life, a baby who would need
All I could give, my love, a home, a name,
My word made flesh though not born of my seed.
Tonight you put your Teddy from your bed –
The magic wanes, the world looms ahead.

Listening to *Desperados Waiting for a Train*

for John

How one thing always leads us to another!
I see you with your granddad once again
As you walk off from your father and your mother
To join him in the world of grown-up men.
And yes, son, local folk called you his sidekick
As you walked around the village hand in hand,
No baby talk, 'twas adult stuff like politics
And it felt good to be treated like a man.
And though granddad's dead and everything is changing,
And you're growing up and soon will leave us, son,
And life's a past we're always rearranging,
When the kid walks with his hero in that song
I see you with your granddad once again
As you walk away to join the world of men.

Sick Child

He's too young to suffer, Lord, like this;
Take this burden from him, make it mine:
I've long put up with troubles; the abyss
I've long looked into. In denying
Whatever it's that troubles him, he pales
And pukes with what the secret won't admit;
Everything the doctors give him fails –
Is there nothing those doctors have can hit
The cause of his strange sickness and can cure
Whatever it's that troubles him this while?
I'd prefer to suffer than endure
Helpless while he suffers. He's my child.
Take this burden from him, hear my plea.
Let me take his load that it unburden me.

Table Quiz

The questions come out neatly one by one.
Son, each one has an answer that's precise;
No room for thinking here as, like a gun,
The mind fires out the answers. Here a voice
Whispers loud its knowledge like a boast,
All that can be known for certain's here:
There are winners, there are losers as we toast
A world where each question's answered clear,
A world where simplicity prevails.
Outside this circle nothing's answered thus,
This futile show of certainty that fails
Every decent question asked of us.
So spit out all the answers while you can
Before the questions come that make a man.

To My Son as He Leaves Home

Son, just to have you 'round the house is good,
The way you make your presence felt. I'll miss
The way that being with you was drink and food;
The future beckons, now it's come to this.
You're leaving, son, I wish you all the best,
May every good that life can give be yours,
Stand firm, love, when life becomes a test,
Remember that the good you do endures.
You're leaving, son, take all you need from me,
It's freely given as it was when you
Needed me, a baby on my knee,
Needed me as to a man you grew.
I love you son, I shed a happy tear
As I let you go, in faith and hope and fear.

To My Daughter, Pregnant

She brings me eggs from chickens she has reared,
Cabbages and carrots she has grown,
All the things about her for which I feared
Have come to naught: she's come into her own.
She brings me eggs from chickens she has reared,
Soon she'll be a mother. I rejoice.
Daughter, from the moment you appeared,
You gave me songs to sing in joyful voice.
Soon you'll be a mother and you'll give
Not eggs just but a grandchild to adore,
Another reason for a man to live
For a grandchild adds its blessings to our store.
Pregnant with the life in which you bloom,
You bless us with the child within your womb.

On Becoming a Grandfather

for Katie Margaret Crowley

I thought I loved until you came along,
No other love can now become a threat,
Love is faithful or everything goes wrong,
There's nothing I have loved that I regret.
I thought I loved until you came along,
You freed me up to be myself, and now
That I've found my voice again in song,
I sing with all that heaven will allow.
I thought I loved until you came along,
The ghosts that haunted me I now call friend,
I love all that I hid for far too long,
When I think of you, Kate, all my old hurts mend.
Never have I known a peace so strong;
I thought I loved until you came along.

My Girlfriends Now Are Other Children's Mamas

My girlfriends now are other children's mamas,
They've married well or broken up in pain,
The love we shared no one can now take from us,
For that alone I'd do it all again.
My girlfriends now are other's children's mamas,
Love let us down, oh! what a price we paid,
And yet we're friends (we never were piranhas),
Of all those loves my wife's the one who stayed.
My girlfriends now are other's children's mamas,
I think of them sometimes with deep regret,
We're older now, sensible as pyjamas,
We still are friends though we're apart, and yet
I pray for them and hope that life will bless
Those early loves that ended in a mess.

Sonnet to Brenda

I won't compare you to a summer's day,
The beaches all deserted in the rain –
Some way, this, to spend a holiday
(You're sorry now you didn't book for Spain).
No! The weather can't be trusted in these parts –
It's fickle as a false love's said to be;
I could get sentimental about hearts
But that's not my style. Poetry,
The only thing that's constant in my life,
The only thing I know that still is true
As my love remains for you, dear wife –
This, then, is what I'll compare to you.
The iambic heart that pulses in these lines
Measures out my love. And it still rhymes.

Just To Be Beside You Is Enough

Just to be beside you is enough,
Just to make your breakfast tea and toast,
To help you with the ware, that kind of stuff,
Just to get the papers and your post;
To hold you in my arms in calm embrace,
Just to sit beside you at the fire,
Just to trace my fingers on your face
Is more to me than all of youth's desire;
Just to lie beside you in the night,
To hear you breathe in peace before I sleep,
To wake beside you in the morning light
In the love we sowed together that we reap.
Together we have taken smooth and rough.
Just to be beside you is enough.

A Valentine In Recessionary Times

Saint Valentine's Day, 2013

My love, I can't afford a valentine,
I've just enough to buy the things we need,
No spare cash to buy you flowers or wine,
I show my love today in word and deed.
Once I bought you valentines that showed
An early love, lavish, insecure,
But, now we've travelled farther down that road,
I know our love is solid, steadfast, sure.
The world has changed since our first valentine,
In the grip of recession now we strive
With misfortune not of our design
And, thus, today I've nothing left to give
But these words; love, take them as a sign
Of all we are, all the days I live.

The Teacher

for David Mason

I wish away my life until the pension
Hoping that, just once, I will connect
With sympathy that is beyond attention;
Instead I keep good order, earn respect.
Once I had a vision for my village –
I'd bring to it a gift of poetry;
Tonight the talk's of quotas and of tillage
And how the barmaid gives out beer for free.
And yet, I've not lost hope in my own people –
My vision was at fault; these people need
To sing and dance, get drunk below the steeple
That accuses them of gossip and of greed.
I mind their children, give them right of way
Into a world I've seen and try to say.

On Being Appointed Principal Teacher of Moyvane National School

For my people who walked barefoot miles to school,
For the children in the years of hand-down dress,
For the hurt who can't forget being branded 'fool',
For the ones who left this parish to success;
For the youths that died in foreign wars, who fought
When adopted lands conscripted them, and those
Who lived and died for Ireland, those who wrought
A nation from a peasant's ragged clothes;
For those who perished homeless, those who took
Their lives in desperation, and for all
Who were wronged or felt diminished by the book,
For those who heard and followed its great call;
For all my predecessors have set free
From the days of the hedge school down to me,
I accept this post.

Before the Word 'Fuck' Came to Common Use

Before the word 'fuck' came to common use
(Even toddlers going to playschool know it now),
Before the lid was raised on child abuse,
We said that we were innocent. But how?
We heard the whispers and we went along
Protecting those who were above the law
In a world we eulogise ('knew right from wrong'),
A world nostalgia paints without a flaw.
Before the word 'fuck' came to common use
We were children and our masters ran the show . . .
Guilty as condemned, it's no excuse
To plead that in the past we didn't know.
Before the word 'fuck' came to common use
Children mattered less than their abusers.

Would You Believe

for Mark Patrick Hederman

Would You Believe on TV Sunday night,
'The Church in Crisis' the subject of debate;
I watch it in the pub, my Church's plight,
'The Pope's a Nazi' one drinker snorts in hate.
Everyone here is Catholic; some object
That they come to the pub for company and chat,
Or else a show with which they can connect,
They don't approve what this poor pilgrim's at.
I go to the loo, the channel's changed
To football – religion's turned them off
(The new religion's sport, I don't complain
As I struggle with my Church, let who will scoff),
Catholics ignoring this debate:
The future of their Church. Too late. Too late.

A Catholic Speaks Out

I'm through with cover-ups, I'm through with Rome,
To think that I believed them all these years,
From now on I'll worship God at home
And bid an end to all my childish fears,
Fears I learned in school where we were crammed
With all the shit the men in black prescribed,
Anyone who questioned them was damned,
They raised their poisoned cup and we imbibed.
I'm through with cover-ups, I'm through with Rome,
The thought police can't reach me now I'm free,
And though I love the art of spire and dome,
The ritual and all it means to me,
I'm through with cover-ups, I'm through with Rome,
From now on I'll worship God at home.

In Extremis

They come to Mass, these kids who never come,
For their friend who took his life eight years ago,
Tonight's the night he'd have been twenty-one,
And still they feel the awful, shocking blow.
Tonight's the night he'd have been twenty-one,
A party night, instead they go to Mass,
Later of course they'll drink and smoke, have fun –
Anything they can to make time pass.
Later these kids will drink and smoke, have fun,
But first they go to Mass, that's what you do
When everything about you's on the run,
Even though your Church is damaged too.
Being here's the scraping of the pot
But, God Almighty man, it's all they've got.

Knockanure Church

A place of worship, simple and austere;
'Sixties architecture past its date.
I wonder what it is that draws me here
To a building local people seem to hate.
The church of their affection, knocked, made way
For the 'garage on the hill' in its design –
Bare brick, flat roof, no steeple, here I pray.
The spirit of this building's kin to mine.

My God's a God who strips me in this place –
No cover here, the lines are stark and spare;
Through the years, I've grown into this space
Where work of human hands raised art to prayer,
The same the builders raised up once at Chartres,
But plainer here, an answer to my heart.

On Hearing Johnny Cash's
American Recordings

The great ones have the courage to believe,
The courage to go naked if so called,
To pare life back to where things don't deceive;
Let those ashamed of feeling be appalled,
Those simple songs of love and death ring true
In an age when we're afraid to show the heart –
'Whatever you say, say nothing', this in lieu
Of a creed that years ago joined prayer and art.
We say nothing and mean nothing now that we
Lose belief and, cynics in our loss,
Look down on the believer, this poetry –
The gospel of a soul that takes its cross,
Songs a life has earned or else are trash,
Salvation, suffered, sung by Johnny Cash.

Homage to Thomas MacGreevy

MacGreevy, poet, Catholic, you found your place
In a world where art redeemed, the word was true,
In a creed that raised living into grace
As, a poet and a Catholic, I must too.
The life a Catholic has to face
Is no different to the life we all go through,
Losing heart at the squalid commonplace
But for a vision that redeems its ugly hue.
So welcome, then, the hopeless and the base,
The depths descended as their artists drew
Their Christs amid dejection and disgrace,
Christ my muse in poem, in pub, in pew.
With MacGreevy, poet, Catholic, I find my place
In a creed that raises living into grace.

Books By Gabriel Fitzmaurice

Poetry in English

Rainsong (Beaver Row Press, Dublin, 1984)
Road to the Horizon (Beaver Row Press, 1987)
Dancing Through (Beaver Row Press, 1990)
The Father's Part (Story Line Press, Oregon, 1992)
The Space Between: New and Selected Poems 1984-1992 (Cló Iar-Chonnachta, Conamara, 1993)
The Village Sings (Story Line Press; Cló Iar-Chonnachta; Peterloo Poets, Cornwall, 1996)
A Wrenboy's Carnival: Poems 1980-2000 (Wolfhound Press, Dublin, Peterloo Poets, 2000)
I and the Village (Marino Books, Dublin, 2002)
The Boghole Boys (Marino Books, Cork, 2005)
Twenty-One Sonnets (Salmon Poetry, Cliffs of Moher, 2007)
The Essential Gabriel Fitzmaurice (Mercier Press, Cork, 2008)
In Praise of Football (Mercier Press, 2009)
Poems of Faith and Doubt (Salmon Poetry, 2011)

Poetry in Irish

Nocht (Coiscéim, Dublin, 1989)
Ag Síobshiúl Chun An Rince (Coiscéim, 1995)

Giolla na nAmhrán: Dánta 1988-1998 (Coiscéim, 1998)

Children's Poetry in English

The Moving Stair (The *Kerryman*, Tralee, 1989)
The Moving Stair (enlarged edition, Poolbeg Press, Dublin, 1993)
But Dad! (Poolbeg Press, 1995)
Puppy and the Sausage (Poolbeg Press, 1998)
Dear Grandad (Poolbeg Press, 2001)
A Giant Never Dies (Poolbeg Press, 2002)
The Oopsy Kid (Poolbeg Press, 2003)
Don't Squash Fluffy (Poolbeg Press, 2004)
I'm Proud to be Me (Mercier Press, 2005)
Really Rotten Rhymes (Mercier Press, 2007)
GF Woz Ere (Mercier Press, 2009)
Splat (Mercier Press, 2012)

Children's Poetry in Irish

Nach Iontach Mar Atá (Cló Iar-Chonnachta, 1994)

Children's Poetry in English and Irish

Do Teachers Go to the Toilet?/An dTéann Múinteoirí go Tigh an Asail? (Mercier Press, 2010)

Essays

Kerry on my Mind (Salmon Publishing, Cliffs of Moher, 1999)
Beat the Goatskin Till the Goat Cries (Mercier Press, 2006)

Translation

The Purge (A translation of *An Phurgóid* by Mícheál Ó hAirtnéide) (Beaver Row Press, 1989)

Poems I Wish I'd Written: Translations from the Irish (Cló Iar-Chonnachta, 1996)

The Rhino's Specs/Spéaclaí an tSrónbheannaigh: Selected Children's Poems of Gabriel Rosenstock (Mercier Press, 2002)

Poems from the Irish: Collected Translations (Marino Books, 2004)

Ventry Calling (Mercier Press, 2005)

House, Don't Fall on Me (Mercier Press, 2007)

Lucinda Sly: The Last Woman Hanged (Liberties Press, 2013)

Editor

The Flowering Tree/An Crann Faoi Bhláth (contemporary poetry in Irish with verse translations) with Declan Kiberd (Wolfhound Press, 1991)

Between the Hills and Sea: Songs and Ballads of Kerry (Oidhreacht, Ballyheigue, 1991)

Con Greaney: Traditional Singer (Oidhreacht, 1991)

Homecoming/ An Bealach 'na Bhaile: Selected poems of Cathal Ó Searcaigh (Cló Iar-Chonnachta, 1993)

Irish Poetry Now: Other Voices (Wolfhound Press, 1993)

Kerry Through Its Writers (New Island Books, Dublin, 1993)

The Listowel Literary Phenomenon: North Kerry Writers: A Critical Introduction (Cló Iar-Chonnachta, 1994)

Rusty Nails and Astronauts: A Wolfhound Poetry Anthology (Wolfhound Press, 1999) with Robert Dunbar

'The Boro' and 'The Cross': The Parish of Moyvane-Knockanure (The Moyvane-Knockanure Millennium Book Committee,

2000) with Áine Cronin and John Looney
The Kerry Anthology (Marino Books, 2000)
'Come All Good Men and True': Essays from the John B. Keane Symposium (Mercier Press, 2004)
The World of Bryan MacMahon (Mercier Press, 2005)

Biographical Note

Gabriel Fitzmaurice was born, in 1952, in the village of Moyvane, County Kerry, where he still lives. For over thirty years he taught in the local primary school, from which he retired as principal in 2007. He is author of more than fifty books, including collections of poetry in English and Irish as well as several collections of verse for children. He has translated extensively from the Irish and has edited a number of anthologies of poetry in English and Irish. He has published two volumes of essays and collections of songs and ballads. Poems of his have been set to music and recorded by Brian Kennedy and RTÉ Cór an nÓg with the RTÉ National Symphony Orchestra. He frequently broadcasts on radio and television on education and the arts.

He has been described as 'the best contemporary, traditional, popular poet in English' in *Booklist* (US), 'a wonderful poet' in the *Guardian*, 'one of Ireland's leading poets' in *Books Ireland*, 'Ireland's favourite poet for children' in *Best Books!* and 'the Irish A. A. Milne' by Declan Kiberd in the *Sunday Tribune*.